Contents

March 24, 2015

The Honorable Patrick Meehan
House of Representatives

Dear Mr. Meehan:

The 1995 bombing of the Alfred P. Murrah Federal Building in Oklahoma City, Oklahoma, the September 11, 2001 terrorist attacks, and more recently, the 2013 shooting at the Washington Navy Yard, in Washington, D.C., have heightened the awareness of, and demonstrated the continued need for, physical security at federal facilities. Since September 11, 2001, federal entities have made improvements to the physical security of their buildings—such as installing blast resistant windows, installing facility exterior barriers, and increasing the number of guards who patrol federal facilities—that have incurred additional costs to the federal government. These entities have also incorporated physical security into the standards and design requirements for new construction and leased facilities. In general, the total costs to the federal government for these enhancements are not known because there are no government-wide data that would allow for tracking them.

GAO has designated federal real property management as a high-risk area for several reasons, including that federal entities continue to face challenges in securing real property and using a risk management strategy to allocate resources.[1] The Interagency Security Committee (ISC),[2] which is chaired by the Department of Homeland Security (DHS) and has representation from across federal civilian entities, has a risk management standard that federal executive-branch entities are to follow.[3] The standard outlines elements essential to effective resource

---

[1] GAO, *High Risk Series: An Update,* GAO-13-283 (Washington D.C.: February 2013).

[2] The ISC was established in 1995 by Executive Order No. 12977, 60 Fed. Reg. 54411 (Oct. 24, 1995), to enhance the quality and effectiveness of security and the protection of buildings and facilities in the United States occupied by federal employees for nonmilitary activities. Executive Order No. 12977 was later amended by Executive Order No. 13286, 68 Fed. Reg. 106190 (March 5, 2003). The ISC is chaired by the Department of Homeland Security and is comprised of 54 federal agencies and departments.

[3] ISC, *The Risk Management Process for Federal Facilities: An Interagency Security Committee Standard* (Washington, D.C.: August 2013).

management, including implementing the most cost-effective enhancements and establishing a comprehensive program for measuring and testing the effectiveness of physical security programs.[4] You asked us to report on issues related to the cost of physical security enhancements at civilian federal facilities.

This report addresses the following questions:

1. What types of physical security enhancements have selected civilian federal entities made to their facilities since September 11, 2001?

2. How do selected civilian federal entities pay for and track costs of such enhancements, and what are the factors that drive those costs?

3. What actions have selected civilian federal entities taken to manage costs, including determining the cost-effectiveness of enhancements and using performance measures?

This report is a public version of a previously issued report identified by DHS and the Department of Justice (DOJ) as containing information designated as For Official Use Only, information that must be protected from public disclosure. Therefore, this report omits sensitive information regarding specific building information and the names and locations of the buildings we visited, among other things. However, the information provided in this report addresses the same questions as the For Official Use Only report, and the overall methodology used for both reports is the same.

To address the questions above, we selected five entities that (1) hold—and manage the security of— their facilities; (2) lease facilities through GSA and rely on security provided at those facilities; or (3) provide security services for building tenants. These entities implemented physical security enhancements at federal facilities since September 11, 2001. The entities we selected include: the Department of Homeland Security's (DHS) Federal Emergency Management Agency (FEMA); the General Services Administration (GSA); the Department of Justice's United States Marshals Service (USMS); the Smithsonian Institution (Smithsonian); and the Social Security Administration (SSA). We selected USMS because it has the primary responsibility for protecting the

---

[4]ISC, *The Risk Management Process for Federal Facilities: An Interagency Security Committee Standard* (August 2013).

judiciary, and the judiciary is one of GSA's largest tenants. At each of the five entities selected, we interviewed officials at the entities' headquarters and field levels and conducted site visits at selected facilities. We selected 10 facilities based on various considerations, including whether they had been renovated or constructed since September 11, 2001, or provided examples of challenges or leading practices of cost management.[5] We also collected and reviewed available security-cost data for security enhancements that were implemented at these facilities since September 11, 2001. In addition, we examined documentation on the management of physical security across their facilities, including entities' policies, guidance, and reports on security and asset management and memorandums of understanding describing security stakeholders' roles and responsibilities. Additionally, we interviewed officials from the Office of Management and Budget (OMB) and the Interagency Security Committee (ISC); and reviewed pertinent laws, policies, and other documents related to security cost management. The information obtained during the site visits and interviews is not generalizable and cannot be used to represent the opinions of all agency officials. We used the information from these site visits and interviews to provide illustrative examples throughout our report. We also reviewed previous GAO work on the issue of security cost management. See appendix I for more details on our scope and methodology.

We conducted this performance audit from January 2014 to March 2015 in accordance with generally accepted government auditing standards. Those standards require that we plan and perform the audit to obtain sufficient, appropriate evidence to provide a reasonable basis for our findings and conclusions based on our audit objectives. We believe the evidence obtained provides a reasonable basis for our findings and conclusions based on our audit objectives.

Background

Physical security for federal facilities has been a heightened government-wide concern since the 1995 bombing of the Alfred P. Murrah Federal Building in Oklahoma City, Oklahoma. After this incident and in response to a presidential directive, DOJ assessed the vulnerability of federal office buildings and identified minimum-security standards.[6] In a memorandum[7]

---

[5]We visited 8 of these facilities and interviewed facility officials at all 10.

[6]DOJ, USMS, *Vulnerability Assessment of Federal Facilities*, (1995).

issued in conjunction with the DOJ study, the President directed executive branch departments and entities to upgrade the security of their facilities using the DOJ standards. We have previously reported on the types of enhancements that civilian federal entities have made to improve physical security at their facilities, such as searching vehicles that enter federal facilities, restricting parking, and installing concrete bollards[8] and security cameras.[9] Entities' physical security programs address how they approach aspects of physical security for their buildings, such as conducting risk assessments to identify threats and vulnerabilities and determine which enhancements to implement.[10] We previously found that entities develop these programs using a variety of information sources such as institutional knowledge or subject matter expertise in physical security, federal statutes and regulations, and federal standards. Entities then tailor these programs to their missions, the types of facilities they occupy, and other circumstances, such as the level of public access needed.[11]

Available data show that in fiscal year 2013, federal civilian entities were responsible for protecting approximately 150,000 buildings. GSA holds or leases over 8,700 of these buildings, which include prominent federal facilities such as agency headquarters office buildings, federal courthouses, and land ports of entry that are accessed by millions of

---

[7]U.S. President (Clinton), "Memorandum on Upgrading Security at Federal Facilities," *Public Papers of the Presidents of the United States*, vol. I, June 28, 1995, 964-965.

[8]Bollards are short, vertical posts that may be fixed or retractable and are generally used to surround a facility as vehicle barriers.

[9]GAO, *General Services Administration: Many Building Security Upgrades Made But Problems Have Hindered Program Implementation*, GAO/T-GGD-98-141 (Washington, D.C.: June 1998); GAO, *Building Security: Security Responsibilities for Federally Owned and Leased Facilities*, GAO-03-8 (Washington, D.C.: October 2002); GAO, *Homeland Security: Further Actions Needed to Coordinate Federal Agencies' Facility Protection Efforts and Promote Key Practices*, GAO-05-49 (Washington, D.C.: November 2004); and GAO, *Homeland Security: Actions Needed to Improve Security Practices at National Icons and Parks*, GAO-09-983 (Washington, D.C.: August 2009).

[10]We have previously reported that because of the considerable differences in types of federal facilities and the variety of risks associated with each of them, there is no single, ideal approach to physical security. GAO, *Building Security: Security Responsibilities for Federally Owned and Leased Facilities*, GAO-03-8 (Washington, D.C.: October 2002).

[11]GAO, *Facility Security: Greater Outreach by DHS on Standards and Management Could Benefit Federal Agencies*, GAO-13-222 (Washington, D.C.: January 2013).

federal employees and visitors.[12] See table 1 for examples of properties included in the portfolio of some of the federal entities we reviewed.

Table 1: Properties Used by Select Federal Entities, 2014

Federal entity	Approximate buildings used	Additional details
Federal judiciary, protected by the United States Marshals Service	440	Federal courthouses, all of which are held and/or leased by the General Services Administration (GSA), range from small court spaces in post offices that may be used on a part-time basis, to large buildings in major urban areas.
Social Security Administration (SSA)	1,300-1,400[a]	The majority of SSA facilities are held and/or leased by GSA, delivering a broad range of services to the general public through a nationwide network of offices, such as regional offices, field offices, card centers, processing centers, and hearing offices.
Smithsonian Institution (Smithsonian)	625	The Smithsonian has multiple facilities including 19 museums and galleries, 20 libraries, 9 research centers, and a zoological park. These facilities contain and provide millions of visitors with access to national collections in American and natural history, art, science, and other areas.
The Department of Homeland Security's Federal Emergency Management Agency (FEMA)	110	FEMA both holds and leases its facilities across the nation; its mission is to support the nation's citizens and first responders to build, sustain and improve our capability to prepare for, protect against, respond to, recover from and mitigate all hazards.[b]

Source: GAO analysis of agency information. | GAO-15-444

[a]SSA officials told us that the agency occupies between 1,300 and 1,400 field offices at any given time, based on relocations and consolidations.

[b]A FEMA headquarters official told us that for leased facilities, FEMA only leases a few facilities itself. Instead, FEMA relies on GSA to lease facilities on behalf of FEMA.

Various entities share in the responsibilities for providing security services at federal facilities, including conducting risk assessments and selecting, implementing, and funding physical security enhancements.[13] For GSA held or leased facilities, DHS's Federal Protective Service (FPS) is the

---

[12]Executive branch departments and agencies subject to the Chief Financial Officers (CFO) Act of 1990 are required to submit real property data at the constructed asset level to the Federal Real Property Profile (FRPP), a federal real property database, on an annual basis. Exec. Order No. 13327, *Federal Real Property Asset Management,* 69 Fed. Reg. 5897 (Feb. 6, 2004). According to fiscal year 2013 FRPP data, non-military CFO Act agencies reported holding nearly 120,000 buildings and leasing close to 30,000 buildings, totaling approximately 150,000 buildings. According to this same data, GSA reported holding nearly 1,600 and leasing over 7,100 buildings, totaling more than 8,700 buildings.

[13]According to the ISC, risk assessments should be conducted at federal facilities on a periodic and timely basis.

GAO-15-444 Homeland SecurityError! Reference source not found.

primary agency responsible for providing law enforcement and related security services, including conducting risk assessments as well as recommending and sometimes implementing physical security enhancements.[14] When an entity has the direct authority to hold or lease non-GSA buildings, the entity is responsible for providing building security and may rely on its own physical security experts or other security organizations, such as FPS or private security companies. Security responsibilities are also shared between or among multiple entities when an entity occupies space in a multi-tenant facility. In these instances, a facility security committee (FSC)[15] is formed and is responsible for making facility-specific security decisions, while entities retain full responsibility for the security in their internal space in the facility.

Security responsibilities at the nation's federal courthouses are a coordinated effort among GSA, FPS, DOJ, USMS, and the Administrative Office of the U.S. Courts (AOUSC)—all of which have some responsibility for the physical security enhancements made at these buildings.[16] Within the federal judiciary, the Judicial Conference of the United States is the principal policy-making body for administering the federal court system, and its Committee on Judicial Security recommends security policies for federal judges and courts.[17] These policies are implemented by AOUSC, which has responsibility for, among other things, monitoring the effectiveness of security programs and use of appropriate funds, coordinating reviews of physical security, and transferring funds to

---

[14]FPS conducts its mission by providing protective security services through two types of activities: (1) physical security activities, such as conducting risk assessments of facilities, providing guard services, and recommending risk-based countermeasures aimed at preventing and reducing the severity of incidents at facilities; and (2) law enforcement activities, such as responding to incidents, conducting criminal investigations, and exercising arrest authority. Under section 1706 of the Homeland Security Act of 2002 (Pub. L. No. 107-296, 116 Stat. 2135, 2138), with authority delegated by the Secretary of Homeland Security, the Under Secretary of National Protection and Programs Directorate may delegate these security responsibilities to the federal entity that holds or leases the space.

[15]A facility security committee consists of representatives from each of the tenant agencies in the facility. The facility security committees are responsible for addressing security issues at their respective facility and approving the implementation of security countermeasures.

[16]A 2004 memorandum of agreement defines the respective roles and responsibilities for court security of GSA, USMS, and AOUSC.

[17]28 U.S.C. § 331.

USMS.[18] USMS has the primary responsibility for the physical security of federal courthouses and, among other security-related activities, conducts security surveys, makes recommendations, and implements physical security enhancements, such as security systems at federal courthouses.[19] Because courthouses are housed in buildings held or leased by GSA, FPS is also responsible for providing certain security services, such as enforcing federal laws and providing building entry and perimeter security.[20] In multi-tenant facilities held or leased by GSA, FPS is also responsible for conducting security surveys and generally is responsible for making physical-security enhancement recommendations for the facility to the FSC. GSA proposes plans for new construction and renovation and is responsible for implementing physical security fixtures in these projects, such as bollards and blast resistant windows at federal courthouses.[21]

Federal entities are not required to report to OMB the total amount they have expended or anticipate expending specifically on physical security enhancements. For instance, OMB collects information for the annual President's budget request from federal entities using 20 major budget functions, such as agriculture, health, and social security, but none of these are specific to any type of security functions. In 2002, legislation was enacted that required OMB to include a homeland-security-funding analysis in the annual President's budget request in an effort to measure federal homeland security expenditures.[22] As a result, OMB requires federal entities to report security expenditures and projected expenditures on such efforts, including those related to homeland security activities. However, to allow flexibility in responses, OMB left the definition of

---

[18]28 U.S.C. § 604.

[19]28 U.S.C. § 566(i).

[20]In 2007, USMS was authorized, in consultation with the Judiciary and FPS, to implement a Perimeter Security Pilot Program for the USMS to assume FPS's responsibilities to provide perimeter security at seven selected courthouses. Consolidated Appropriations Act, 2008. Pub. L. No. 110-161, div. D, title III, § 307, 121 Stat. 1990 (2007). At the time of our report, the pilot program was still in effect.

[21]6 U.S.C. § 232(a).

[22]According to the Homeland Security Act, the term 'homeland security' refers to those activities that detect, deter, protect against, and respond to terrorist attacks occurring within the United States and its territories. Homeland Security Act of 2007, Pub. L. No. 107-296, § 889, 116 Stat. 2135 (2002).

'activity' to the interpretation of respondent entities, and OMB guidance does not specify if physical security enhancements to federal facilities should be included. As such, reported costs may not include all of the costs of physical security enhancements made at federal facilities. OMB has reported that collecting data on homeland security is difficult because entities often do not report these activities distinctly from other programs. Additionally, in 2002, we asked 22 entities to report how much they expended on building security from 1996 to 2001, but found that the level of information varied. Entities told us the reasons for reporting limited cost information included (1) security costs were funded partially by another entity, (2) security costs were part of the lease costs and not separately identified, and (3) security is not a separate line-item for entities' funding.

Although there are no government-wide data available that identify how much entities have expended specifically on physical security, the amount expended on homeland security efforts is significant. For example, for the fiscal–year-2015 President's budget request, civilian federal entities reported to OMB that they expended approximately $50 billion in fiscal year 2013 on homeland security activities and that they anticipated expending over $56 billion and $57 billion in fiscal years 2014 and 2015, respectively, on these activities.[23] In addition, entities also received federal funding for anti-terrorism efforts soon after the attacks on September 11, 2001, to make improvements to the security of federal buildings. On September 18, 2001, Congress appropriated $40 billion to the President in the Fiscal Year 2001 Emergency Supplemental Appropriations Act for Recovery from and Response to Terrorist Attacks on the United States, and $8.6 million of this was transferred to the Federal Buildings Fund, which is administered by GSA, to provide increased security for federal buildings.[24] Also, in the first quarter of fiscal year 2002, GSA received additional funding of $98.5 million for FPS to make security-related improvements at federal buildings.[25]

ISC's mandate is to enhance the quality and effectiveness of security in and protection of federal facilities through activities such as developing

---

[23]According to OMB, these estimates do not include the efforts of the legislative or judicial branches. OMB, *Analytical Perspectives: Budget of the United States Government (Fiscal Year 2015)*.

[24]Pub. L. No. 107-38, 115. Stat. 220 (2001).

[25]FPS was still part of GSA in 2002.

and evaluating security standards for federal facilities, developing a strategy for ensuring compliance with these standards, and overseeing the implementation of appropriate protective security measures in federal facilities, among other things. ISC was created by Executive Order 12977 in 1995, after the bombing of the Alfred P. Murrah federal building in Oklahoma City, Oklahoma, to address physical security across federal facilities occupied by federal employees.[26] From 2008 through 2013, ISC issued a series of standards to assist federal entities in developing and implementing physical security programs. In August 2013, ISC combined six existing ISC standards into a single standard, *The Risk Management Process for Federal Facilities*, which according to ISC, is intended to provide entities with an integrated, single source of physical security information and guidance.[27] The standard directs entities, among other things, to consider whether or not an enhancement can be physically implemented and whether the investment is cost-effective.

Federal Entities Have Implemented a Range of Physical Security Enhancements

The federal civilian entities we selected—FEMA, GSA, USMS, Smithsonian, and SSA—have implemented a range of enhancements to improve physical security since September 11, 2001. Officials from all five of the entities we reviewed told us they used the ISC guidance, supplemented by security policies and recommendations from their facility officials, to help them determine the types of enhancements to implement at their facilities. This is consistent with findings of a 2012 GAO survey of non-military entities, which showed that 21 of the 29 respondents said that ISC guidance largely informs them in determining appropriate enhancements, among other activities.[28] ISC's standard provides entities with an integrated, single source of information on physical security enhancements and recommends the enhancements entities should

---

[26]Initially, ISC was chaired by GSA. The Homeland Security Act of 2002 created DHS, and, in 2003, Executive Order 13286 amended Executive Order 12977 to transfer chairmanship of the ISC from GSA to DHS. 68 Fed. Reg. 10619 (Mar. 5, 2003).

[27]The ISC standard incorporated the following six existing ISC standards: *The Design Basis Threat, Facility Security Level Determinations for Federal Facilities, Use of Physical Security Performance Measures, Physical Security Criteria for Federal Facilities, Facility Security Committees*, and *Child Care Centers Level of Protection Template*.

[28]See GAO-13-222. For this report, we surveyed 32 non-military entities about the sources they use to inform them on how to conduct their physical security programs. Twenty-nine entities responded to the survey question on how ISC standards informed key aspects of physical security.

implement to effectively minimize risk and meet baseline levels of protection at their facilities.[29] The standard identifies six categories of enhancements, described below, that entities may implement at facilities:

- **Site**—including the site perimeter, site access, exterior areas and assets, and parking. Examples include landscaping, signage and lighting, parking access, vehicle barriers and screening.

- **Structure**—including structural hardening, facade, windows, and building systems. Examples include blast resistant windows and façade and protection and placement of ventilation systems and utilities.

- **Facility Entrances**—including employee and visitor pedestrian entrances and exits, loading docks, and other openings in the building envelope. Examples include employee and visitor access control and screening and perimeter doors and locks.

- **Interior**—including space planning and security of specific interior spaces. Examples include space planning, security of critical areas restricted access to nonpublic areas, and protection of interior windows.

- **Security Systems**—including intrusion-detection, access control, and closed-circuit television (CCTV) camera systems. Examples include CCTV monitoring and recording, security control-center, intrusion-detection coverage and monitoring and communication systems.

- **Security Operations and Administration**—including planning, guard force operations, management and decision making, and mail handling and receiving. Examples include security operations management, guards, facility security plan, and employee training.

Officials at all the federal entities in our review told us they have implemented one or more of the enhancements in each of these categories across their portfolio. Figure 1 provides examples of these enhancements at the facilities we visited.

---

[29]According to FEMA headquarters officials, FEMA uses a customized level of protection and not the baseline level of protection mentioned above. The customized level of protection is based on the threat information received from multiple sources utilizing the current guidance.

Figure 1: Examples of Physical Security Enhancements at Selected Federal Facilities

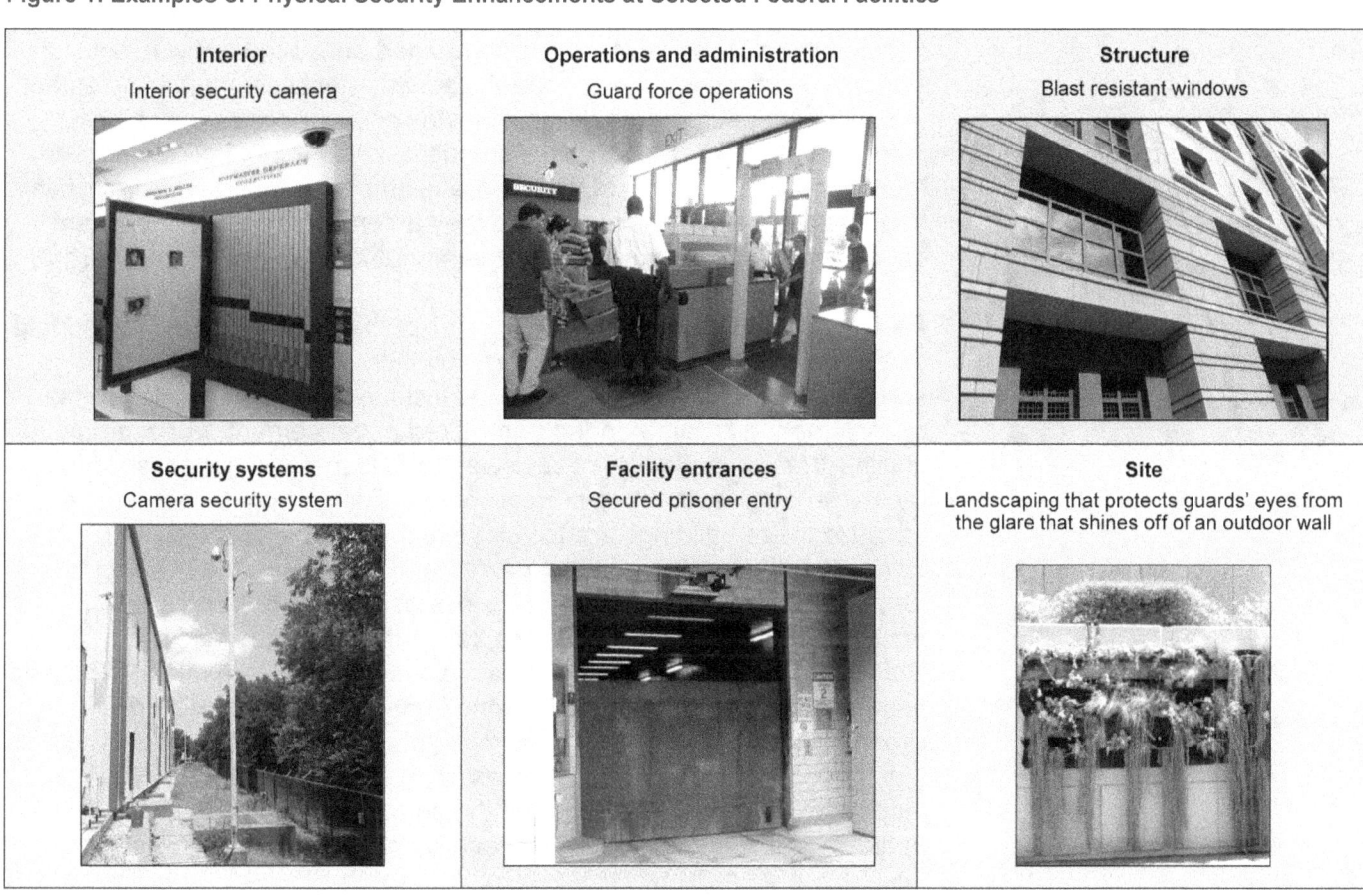

Interior	Operations and administration	Structure
Interior security camera	Guard force operations	Blast resistant windows

Security systems	Facility entrances	Site
Camera security system	Secured prisoner entry	Landscaping that protects guards' eyes from the glare that shines off of an outdoor wall

Source: GAO. | GAO-15-444

The ISC's risk-management process standard also provides entities with guidance on how to customize the security enhancements selected in their facilities. According to the standard, an entity might implement different enhancements for a variety of reasons.[30] The standard also allows for entities to reject or defer the baseline level of protection even if the risks are not mitigated, but agencies must document the reasons for

---

[30]Examples of these reasons can include: site-specific conditions where the recommended baseline level of protection does not fully address the specific risks at the facility; the baseline level of protection cannot be physically implemented; or instances where the enhancement may be cost-prohibitive or not cost-effective.

GAO-15-444 Homeland SecurityError! Reference source not found.

accepting the remaining risk. Officials from four of the five entities told us they have a process by which facility or headquarters officials may document the reasons why a recommended enhancement was not selected. Additionally, the standard states that entities should implement the enhancements required by their own security policies over what is recommended based on the ISC standard, when those policies exceed the ISC minimum standard. Below are examples of the reasons officials from the facilities we visited told us they deferred or did not implement enhancements recommended for their facility based on ISC standards.

Facility Characteristics: Officials from all of the five entities we visited told us that certain types of facility characteristics, such as the location, age, and design of a facility, may make it difficult or even impossible for them to implement a recommended or required enhancement. For example, officials from one agency we reviewed told us that it is not possible to provide enough setback to protect some buildings from blast damage because these buildings are too close to the adjacent roads. Consequently, they accept the risk rather than moving the building to a less urban locale where it would be less accessible to the public. According to four of the entities we selected, there may also be challenges with implementing certain types of enhancements at facilities that have been designated as historic under the National Historic Preservation Act (NHPA). For example, previously, USMS officials told us that, based on NHPA considerations, they did not request that GSA modify the interior layout of one of the courthouses to construct a dedicated judges' elevator and a secured prisoner hallway, which is recommended for U.S. courthouse buildings,[31] because the courthouse has been designated as an historic property under NHPA.[32]

Cost of Enhancements: Officials from all the entities we visited told us that they might not implement certain recommended enhancements because they are too costly. Officials from these entities told us there are some types of enhancements that are more costly than others, such as replacing windows to make them blast resistant. These officials said they might mitigate the risk by implementing other enhancements, defer the implementation of the recommended enhancement, or accept the risk and do nothing. For example, officials at one entity said that they have deferred installing blast resistant windows at some building locations until the replacements could be combined with other large renovation projects already scheduled.

Enhancements Considered Unnecessary: Officials from four of the five entities we visited told us there were instances where they did not concur with the need for a recommended enhancement or believed they had already mitigated the specific risk using different methods. For example, officials from FEMA's Region 6 in Denton, Texas, told us that there were enhancements recommended in their facility's risk assessment that they did not implement. The officials told us that they disagreed with the recommendation because the risk had already been mitigated using alternative methods.

Enhancements Conflict with Mission: Officials from three of the five entities told us there are also instances where they believe the

---

[31]Judicial Conference of the United States, "U.S. Courts Design Guide," 2007. The Judicial Conference of the United States, which serves as the principal policy-making body for the administration of the U.S. Courts, issued this court design guide to address, among other things, heightened security concerns. It describes standards for new construction and leases for courthouses and annexes. It states that judges should have a means to move from a restricted parking area to chambers, as well as to move between chambers, courtrooms, and other spaces through restricted corridors. The guide also states that jurors must be able to move between floors on restricted-access elevators without crossing public spaces or secure prisoner corridors and that the Marshals Service has a means to move prisoners without passing or entering public or restricted spaces.

[32]NHPA requires agencies to manage historic properties in keeping with their historic character, but it does not mandate a particular government decision; instead, it mandates a particular process for reaching a decision. *See* 16 U.S.C. § 470h-2 and GAO, *Federal Real Property: Improved Data Needed to Strategically Manage Historic Buildings, Address Multiple Challenges,* GAO-13-35 (Washington, D.C.: December 2012).

GAO-15-444 Homeland SecurityError! Reference source not found.

implementation of the recommended enhancement would conflict with the entities' mission. For example, officials from the SSA and Smithsonian both said that they must select enhancements that balance the need to maintain safety, while making their facilities easily accessible to the public.[33] They said they would sometimes adjust recommended enhancements that make it difficult to maintain open access to the public.

FSC Process: Officials from all of the selected entities told us that the FSC process for approving physical security enhancements could result in the rejection or the delay of a recommended enhancement. As discussed earlier, FSCs are formed when there are multiple tenants located in a building, and the FSC has the responsibility for making decisions on the types of physical security enhancements to be implemented to the exterior and common spaces of the building. Each entity in a facility has a weighted vote—based on the amount of space the entity occupies—on whether or not to implement and fund recommended enhancements. We have previously found that the FSC structure may not contribute to effective protection of federal facilities in some cases. For example, the entities' representatives to the FSC may not have the security expertise to make risk-based decisions or the authority to commit their respective entities to fund security enhancements and they may find the enhancement too expensive.[34] USMS officials told us that in some buildings, the FSC members may not understand the importance of implementing an enhancement and may instead approve a cosmetic upgrade to the building. Similarly, Smithsonian officials also told us that the FSC process may affect the enhancements made at a building, telling us the FSCs at the multi-tenant buildings where the Smithsonian occupies space have rejected and delayed approving enhancements recommended by FPS.

Enhancements Exceeding Minimum Standards: Officials at four of five of the entities we visited also told us there are instances where they will implement enhancements that exceed what is recommended by the ISC. For example, SSA officials told us that they have implemented physical security enhancements at their facilities that exceed ISC's

---

[33]We have previously found that, in protecting federal buildings, it is a challenge to balance increased security with the public's access to government offices for services and to transact other business. See GAO-05-790.

[34]GAO-10-236T and GAO-10-901.

recommendations, such as requiring that all of their buildings have duress alarms,[35] closed-circuit television (CCTVs), intrusion detection systems, and armed guards. The officials said they took these steps in response to an increase in the number of threats to their employees and enhanced concerns about active shooters. In addition, USMS told us they have implemented enhancements beyond what is recommended in ISC guidance for courthouses where certain types of civil and criminal cases pose increased security risks, such as those involving domestic and international terrorism, domestic and international organized crime, drug trafficking, extremist groups, and gangs. For example, at one courthouse we visited, USMS officials told us that they implemented temporary, additional security enhancements in preparation for a major terrorist trial, such as closing nearby roads, constructing additional entry barriers, and increasing guard presence.

Federal Entities Use Various Funding Vehicles, and Several Factors Drive Physical Security Costs

Entities Use Various Means to Fund Enhancements and Track Enhancement Costs Differently

The federal entities we selected —FEMA, GSA, USMS, Smithsonian, and SSA—used various means of funding to pay for physical security enhancements in their facilities and for some of these types of funding, entities do not track or are not provided with cost information for enhancements, making it difficult for them to identify the total amount expended on enhancements in their facilities. We found that entities choose how they fund enhancements depending on a number of factors, such as: (1) whether the entity holds or leases the facility; (2) the organization at the facility that is responsible for implementing the

---

[35]Duress alarm systems must be installed in SSA offices that deal with the public. Each reception window, interviewing workstation, private interview room, and hearing room must have an operational duress alarm button to activate the system and alert management, the guard, or other employees of a disruptive incident requiring assistance.

enhancement; (3) the project type, such as new construction or renovation; and (4) availability of funding provided to the entity. Table 2 includes examples of the methods entities used to pay for enhancements in categories that we created based on the descriptions provided to us by the entities. Entities may refer to these means of funding in different ways.

Table 2: Examples of Methods Used by Selected Entities to Pay for Security Enhancements

Funding method	Description
Rent payments	All of the entities in our review leased space, such as through the General Services Administration (GSA), and may pay for some physical security enhancements through their rent. For example, for facilities leased through GSA, security enhancements that are either part of a building or attached to the building and are not easily removed and some types of security equipment may be amortized as part of the rent.[a] For instance GSA implemented a $3.2-million window-glazing project at one of its buildings in 2003 and will pass on these costs to any of the tenants in the building for the next 20 years.
Security fees or contracts	All five of the entities in our review told us they pay security organizations, such as the Federal Protective Service (FPS) or private security companies, to install, operate, or maintain physical security enhancements, such as screening services and security systems, through security fees or contracts.
Lump sum payments to lessors and security organizations	Entities may also use reimbursable agreements to pay GSA and FPS to implement and maintain specific types of enhancements at facilities that are beyond the enhancements already provided at the building. For example, Social Security Administration (SSA) officials at the headquarters location in Woodlawn, Maryland, told us they are paying GSA to construct a new control room using a lump sum payment that will not be amortized into the rent.
Funding designated for Renovation or new construction projects	Officials at four of the five entities we selected told us they paid for physical security enhancements that were implemented during a renovation or new construction using funding designated specifically for that project. For example, in 2013, GSA officials told us they completed a renovation to their headquarters building using designated funding, which included installing vehicle bollards, blast resistant windows, and electronic security systems, such as cameras, turnstiles, electronic card readers.
Funding designated for entity-wide security projects	Two of the five entities we selected told us they might pay for enhancements to be implemented across their portfolio through funding allocated for an entity-wide security project.
General security funding designated for enhancements	Officials from four of the entities we selected told us that they allocate funding for security at their facilities and part of this funding is available for the physical security enhancements that are requested for specific facilities.
Supplemental appropriations provided to entities for specific uses	Three of the entities in our review paid for physical security enhancements through supplemental appropriations. For example, Smithsonian received a Congressional appropriation of almost $22 million in fiscal year 2002 as emergency supplemental funding for anti-terrorism measures at their museums. The funding was used for a number of different activities, including increasing the number of Smithsonian security staff to conduct external patrols and operate magnetometers and X-ray machines and for various types of enhancements at some of their museums.

Source: GAO analysis of agency information. | GAO-15-444

[a]There are three pricing categories that are amortized into the rent for GSA leased facilities, including (1) the Shell Rental Component, which includes the cost of all of the ISC-recommended

enhancements for a FSL I building, (2) the Building Specific Amortized Capital Rental Component includes any costs for enhancements above the costs for enhancements required for a FSL I building, and (3) the Tenant-Specific Security, which only includes security fixture enhancements that are requested by the tenant agency and exceed the level of security required by a risk assessment. FSLs range from security levels I to V and are categorized based on the analysis of several security-related facility factors, which serves as the basis for the implementation of physical security measures specified in ISC standards.

All of the entities we selected told us it would be difficult for them to determine how much they have expended on physical security enhancements across their facilities.[36] As described earlier, in 2002, entities reported having limited information on building security expenditures because (1) security costs were funded partially by another entity; (2) security costs were part of the lease costs and not separately identified; and (3) security is not a separate line-item for entities' funding. According to entity officials in our review, they cannot identify all enhancement costs or are not provided with these costs when using certain means of funding, such as rent payments, security fees, or renovation and new construction funding. For example, although GSA identifies some security expenses that are charged to agencies via building-specific amortized capital fees,[37] entity officials told us that lessors, such as GSA, do not always identify how much of the rent fee is attributable to physical security enhancements.

Additionally, officials told us that the cost of physical security enhancements may be combined with other security costs or non-security related costs when enhancements are implemented during a renovation or new construction, making it difficult to isolate costs specific to physical

---

[36]In its technical comments on a draft of this report, AOUSC said that the judiciary's Court Security appropriation, which funds the USMS-administered Judicial Facility Security Program, has two major elements: security systems/ equipment, and court security officer guarding. The security systems/equipment budget is a discrete part of the overall Judicial Facility Security Program and its funding cannot be used for other purposes without a formal reprogramming request and approval by Congress. The USMS has no other funding source for courthouse security than the JFSP. The Judicial Conference of the United States' Committee on Judicial Security and the AOUSC work closely with the USMS in the formulation and oversight of execution of USMS's security systems/equipment budget. AOUSC also said that FPS has no funding for security systems and equipment other than what tenant agencies agree to support via Facility Security Committees. The judiciary's prorated share of such costs is also borne by the Court Security appropriation.

[37]These security enhancements include security fixtures installed in the building, such as bollards or window blast mitigation.

security enhancements. For example, Smithsonian officials told us that they may renovate a museum and part of the renovation would include replacing a wall. While the main purpose of renovating and replacing the wall may not be for security reasons, they will build the wall to meet security standards. The additional cost to meet that requirement is not easily identifiable. Additionally, they said that improvements to physical security may be necessary when completing a different type of security project, such as upgrading information technology systems, and whether the costs should be attributable to improving physical security or some other type of physical upgrade is not always clear. However, officials from the entities we selected told us they can identify costs for enhancements when they pay for these through other types of funding means, such as when they pay an individual lump-sum payment to a lessor or security organization or when individual enhancement projects are approved and paid for through general funding allocated for security. Table 3 provides an example of the means of funding SSA has used to pay for enhancements and its ability to track all of the costs of the enhancements implemented across all of its buildings.

Table 3: Social Security Administration's Means of Funding and Ability to Track Costs of Physical Security Enhancements Made across Its Facilities

Funding method	Description	Costs identifiable?
General Services Administration (GSA) Rent Payments	The Social Security Administration's (SSA) rent to GSA may include the costs for enhancements they make to the facility, which are then amortized into the rent payment.	No: SSA officials cannot identify the enhancement costs because they are not itemized in the rent bill.
Federal Protective Service (FPS) Security Fees via Administration Account	SSA pays for the security enhancements provided by FPS through annual security fees.	No: The security bill FPS provides SSA does not break out the costs of enhancements and SSA officials would not be able to identify specific costs.[a]
Lump Sum Payments to GSA and FPS	SSA may pay GSA and FPS lump sum reimbursable payments to implement specific physical security enhancements.	Yes: SSA officials can identify these costs.
Funding Designated for Renovation or New Construction Projects	SSA uses this funding to pay for security enhancements that are made during renovation and new construction projects.	Maybe: SSA may or may not be able to track these costs.
Entity-wide Physical Security Projects	SSA has separate funding for entity-wide physical security projects.	Yes: SSA can identify these costs.
General Security Funding Designated for Enhancements	SSA uses this funding to pay for enhancements, such as individual enhancements requested by facility officials, based on recommendations from assessments or observed need.	Yes: SSA officials can track costs for enhancements paid with this type of funding.
Appropriations Provided to Entities for Specific Uses	SSA pays a private security guard company through an annual contract for their guard services.	Yes: SSA can identify those contract costs.

Source: GAO analysis based on SSA information. | GAO-15-444

[a]In response to our draft report, FPS headquarters officials said that FPS provides itemized billing by building that includes: (1) basic security charges; (2) building specific charges for countermeasures; and (3) security work authorizations requested for specific measures.

As discussed earlier, OMB does not require that federal entities report physical security costs separately, but as part of their homeland-security mission's funding requirements. Under these requirements, OMB allows entities flexibility on what can be reported as expenditures on homeland security. Nevertheless, as the above examples illustrate, it can often be difficult to isolate physical security costs.

Several Factors Drive the Costs of Enhancements

Officials from the entities we selected described several factors that may increase or decrease the amount they expend on physical security enhancements at their facilities. Below are examples of some of the factors identified by the entities we selected.[38]

Facility Security Level: ISC guidelines established a baseline set of physical security countermeasures to be applied to all federal facilities based on the designated facility security level (FSL).[39] Officials from two entities told us that facilities with higher facility security levels require more enhancements with greater security features, which drives the cost for enhancements at that facility. Therefore, an entity will likely expend more on enhancements at buildings with higher FSLs.

Facility Characteristics: Officials from all of the entities we selected told us that enhancement costs also depend on a number of site-specific and facility-related factors, such as the geographic location of a building, age and size of the facility, historical designation, or whether significant infrastructure changes would be needed to implement the enhancement. For example, GSA officials said that facilities that are setback from the road may have less need for some risk-mitigation enhancements, thereby a decrease in the amount expended on enhancements at the facility. Officials from two of the entities we selected told us that installing bollards at some facilities were more expensive than at other facilities because they are located in Washington, D.C., and needed to meet the aesthetic design recommendations of the National Capital Planning Commission.[40] See figure 2 for examples of the more expensive bollards below.

---

[38]In addition to the examples we provide for the federal executive branch entities we reviewed, AOUSC also said in its technical comments to the report that the costs to federal agencies in trying to implement HSPD-12, and the subsequent and ever-changing executive branch physical access control systems requirements are the most costly aspect of securing federal facilities. AOUSC also said that life-cycle maintenance/management of security systems currently in place is a critical element of facility security costs which requires additional funding.

[39]FSLs range from security levels I to V and are categorized based on the analysis of several security-related facility factors, an analysis that serves as the basis for the implementation of physical security measures specified in ISC standards.

[40]In October 2000, the House and Senate Committees on Appropriations asked the National Capital Planning Commission to provide professional planning advice on federal security measures for the capital with the goal to identify urban design solutions that would set a benchmark for security design throughout the nation's capital.

Figure 2: Bollards in Washington, D.C., Customized to Meet National Capital Planning Commission's Design Recommendations

Specially designed security bollard

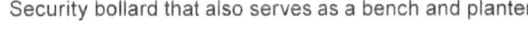

Security bollard that also serves as a bench and planter

Typical security bollard at one location

Typical security bollard at one location

Source: GAO. | GAO-15-444

Officials from facilities we visited told us the structure of a facility might also result in higher costs. For example, an official from the FSC at one of the buildings we visited told us that installing card readers into the walls of the facility was more expensive than at other facilities because the walls were made of marble and they needed to remove asbestos prior to installation. Additionally, officials from an entity we reviewed told us that the window frames at one of their buildings could not accommodate the weight of certain blast resistant windows and caused facility officials to select an alternative solution.

Project Type: Officials from four of the entities we selected told us that it is generally less expensive to implement physical security enhancements in new construction projects rather than during renovations. For example, GSA officials said that renovations often require retrofitting pre-existing building structures to accommodate the enhancements, which would not be necessary when implementing those enhancements in new construction. Similarly, Smithsonian officials said that installing blast resistant windows to pre-existing buildings might require the walls to be reconfigured for the windows to fit.

Risk Acceptance: Officials from three of the entities in our review told us that the level of risk they accept will influence the number and type of enhancements, which influences how much is expended on physical security. In some cases, an entity will be more risk averse than the identified needs reported in the risk assessment. For example, SSA officials told us that they require armed guards at all of their facilities, but this enhancement is above what is required by the ISC standard at many of the SSA sites. Although this increases costs significantly, SSA officials told us they consider this cost essential to protecting their facilities, staff, and visitors and maintaining their mission to be open to the general public. As discussed earlier, an entity may also accept the risk identified in the risk assessment and not implement an enhancement, reducing its overall costs.

GAO-15-444 Homeland SecurityError! Reference source not found.

Selected Federal Entities Use a Range of Cost Management Methods, but Face Difficulties in Evaluating Cost-effectiveness and Measuring Performance

Federal Entities Use a Range of Methods to Manage Costs

Officials from the entities we selected both at the headquarters and facility levels described a number of strategies they used to ensure that they implement the most cost-effective physical security enhancements in their facilities. Below are some examples of ways that entities told us they manage their costs.

Selecting Contract Methods: Officials from the headquarters level at three of the five entities we reviewed told us they contract with private security companies to implement, operate, and maintain certain types of enhancements across all of their facilities rather than obtain these services from different vendors at each facility, enabling them to reduce enhancement costs. For example, USMS officials told us they have national contracts with private security companies to install and maintain security equipment such as CCTV equipment, duress alarms, and access control systems. USMS officials said these contracts reduce their costs because they obtain the contractor's services at a competitive price, reducing maintenance and replacement costs.

Coordinating and Deferring Implementation: According to headquarters officials from three of the entities we reviewed, another method they used to manage costs was to coordinate and defer the implementation of multiple enhancements until renovations occur at the targeted facility. For example, officials from one entity we reviewed said that they will defer an approximately $40-million project to install blast resistant windows at one of their buildings until an upcoming renovation, allowing them to make the necessary adjustments to the window walls along with other building enhancements being done to the facade of the building. According to these officials, this approach will save costs and potentially avoid the

GAO-15-444 Homeland SecurityError! Reference source not found.

need to completely close the building. GSA officials told us that some enhancements are easier and more cost-effective to do during building projects that are un-related to physical security. For example, if there is a project planned to upgrade a lobby, it would be cost-efficient to also implement security upgrades at the same time.

Implementing Alternative Enhancements: Headquarters and facility level officials from four of the entities we selected told us that selecting alternative types of physical security enhancements has saved them in costs, but not reduced the level of security in their buildings. For example, GSA officials told us that the cost of security guard services accounts for a large portion of physical security costs at their facilities, as each guard costs approximately $140,000 per year. To reduce these costs, GSA officials are currently reviewing other types of enhancements, such as the installation of additional cameras and motion detector systems that would enable them to reduce the number of guards at facilities. GSA officials told us that they modified guard service at one of their buildings we visited, including shifting guards to different guard stations, rather than acquiring new guards at a new entrance, saving approximately $440,000 annually. SSA officials from one of the buildings we visited told us that in order to reduce their costs for building security, they consider what options and technologies they really need to reduce vulnerabilities and risks at their facilities. For example, to save costs, they told us they may use basic surveillance cameras rather than a high-level camera if there is no need for the features associated with the high-level camera. Alternatively, GSA officials told us at one building, they were able to reduce the number of cameras used and the number of guard rotations outside of the building after installing cameras with advanced technologies.

Assessing Reasonableness: Officials at all five of the entities we selected told us that they informally consider the reasonableness of implementing an enhancement on a case-by-case basis. They told us they examine several factors, such as the potential costs, associated risks, and past performance of similar projects. For example, officials from FEMA's Region 6 facility told us they review how much an enhancement will cost and the vulnerability it is intended to address and make a decision based on "common sense" and discussions with officials as to whether to implement the enhancement.[41] Smithsonian officials told us they assess the reasonableness of proposed enhancements, taking into consideration the risks of not implementing the enhancement, the costs, the impact on museum operations, and whether the implementation of the enhancement will reduce the risk identified.

Selecting from Technically Equivalent Vendors Based on Cost: Officials at five of the facilities we selected told us that they compare and select the vendor offering the lowest prices while still meeting the standards. For example, officials from FEMA's Region 6 Field Office and officials from SSA's Field Office in California told us that they review multiple bids from contractors and that they will typically select the vendor with the lowest price quote that meets their specifications.[42]

Prioritizing Enhancements: Officials from three of the entities we selected also told us that they prioritize the enhancements needed at their facilities. For example, USMS officials told us they have a process for ranking the enhancements recommended at their facilities, including federal courthouses. Officials told us that when USMS district officials make recommendations on the enhancements they need at their facilities, they will designate each enhancement into four different categories—mandatory, compliance, supplemental, and upgrade[43]—which the headquarters office uses when allocating resources across the districts. Smithsonian officials told us they prioritize recommended enhancements based on the Smithsonian's Security Design Standards and the location of the enhancements. For example, they said enhancements made at a collection storage area have priority over an office space and the perimeter of a building has priority over internal spaces.

---

[41]In its technical comments on a draft of this report, DHS said that FEMA utilizes current threat information to base decisions on facts for determining whether to implement countermeasures. The ultimate decision to accept risk or implement a countermeasure comes from the Regional Designated Official as per the ISC guidelines.

[42]According to a FEMA headquarters official, FEMA's Region 6 Field office and FEMA's Office of the Chief Security Officer review quotes together to determine the best value for the government as per the Federal Acquisition Regulation.

[43]USMS defines mandatory as internal facility standards that USMS requires in all space occupied by the courts. Compliance is defined as a priority based on an external source, such as FPS, identifying a deficiency. Supplemental is defined as vulnerabilities identified by USMS once all mandatory and supplemental security requirements have been met. Upgrade is defined as a need to upgrade equipment that is nearing its end-of-life.

ISC Has Emphasized the Importance of Evaluating the Cost-effectiveness of Enhancements and Measuring Performance

In its August 2013 risk management standard, ISC summarizes a process for applying the most cost-effective enhancements appropriate for reducing identified risks and vulnerabilities to an acceptable level. According to ISC, cost-effectiveness is partly based on the investment in the security enhancement versus the value of the asset. For example, the guidance states that if the life-cycle of the asset is almost expired, it may not be cost-effective for an entity to implement an expensive enhancement. To determine the amount of the investment that is cost-effective, the standard specifies that entities use a cost analysis methodology that considers all costs, including direct project costs, indirect impacts,[44] and life-cycle costs. In multi-tenant facilities, the guidance states that the responsible security organization, such as FPS for many of the GSA held and leased spaces, should develop such a cost analysis for proposed enhancements.

As enhancements may compete with other program objectives for funding, the ISC standard also states that entities should establish a comprehensive performance-measurement and testing program that will allow the entity to measure a security program's capabilities and effectiveness, help demonstrate the need to obligate funds for facility security, and make appropriate decisions for allocating resources. The standard states that, to make appropriate resource decisions, entities need information, such as what is being accomplished, what needs attention, and what is performing at target expectation levels. According to the standard, performance measurement activities should involve collaboration between officials at the entity's headquarters and facility levels.

In past reports, we found that analyzing the cost-effectiveness of physical security resources and using performance measures is important. For example, we identified six key practices in facility protection that could provide a framework for guiding entities' efforts and achieving success, including resource allocation using risk management and performance measurement and testing.[45] In other work, we found that entities would

---

[44]Indirect impacts can include items such as business interruption, relocation costs, or road closures.

[45]These practices included, among others, allocating resources using risk management, including determining cost-effective resources, leveraging cost-effective technologies, and using performance measurement and testing to ensure accountability for achieving broad program goals and improved security at the individual facility level. GAO-05-49.

benefit from using performance measures for physical security in a number of ways, including their use to evaluate the effectiveness of physical security programs, to prioritize security needs, and to justify investment decisions so that an entity can maximize available resources. For example, entities could use security assessments and other active testing to test security initiatives. This step could include testing security equipment such as perimeter alarms and x-ray machines, and conducting simulated attacks and penetration exercises on a periodic basis.[46] As part of these efforts, we recommended that the ISC establish key practices, guidance, and standards for measuring performance in facility protection. The ISC subsequently issued guidance on using physical security performance measures in 2009,[47] and in 2013, ISC consolidated multiple guidance documents, including its 2009 performance measures guidance, into its risk management standard.[48]

Selected Entities Face Difficulties Implementing the Cost-effectiveness and Performance Measurement Aspects of the ISC Standard

The ISC standard states that entities should use a cost analysis methodology that considers all costs, including direct project costs, indirect impacts, and life-cycle costs in making security investment decisions. While this is positive and represents a rigorous approach to determining cost-effectiveness, the ISC standard does not provide detailed guidance or specify a methodology an entity should use to implement this part of the standard. Officials from the selected entities said they have had difficulty implementing the cost-effective part of the ISC standard to the degree that is specified by ISC. Instead, the entities told us that they make their decisions based on various methods such as developing a menu of possible countermeasures and determining their costs and possible trade-offs, reviewing past reports to see if there is precedence for acquiring the enhancement, and using "common sense" and information from facility officials. Officials from GSA, SSA, Smithsonian, USMS, and FEMA agreed it would be beneficial for the ISC

---

[46]GAO-05-49 and GAO, *Homeland Security: Guidance and Standards Are Needed for Measuring the Effectiveness of Agencies' Facility Protection Efforts*, GAO-06-12 (Washington, D.C.: May 2006).

[47]DHS, *Interagency Security Committee Use of Physical Security Performance Measures* (2009).

[48]ISC, *The Risk Management Process for Federal Facilities: An Interagency Security Committee Standard* (August 2013).

to provide them with further guidance or examples of how to implement this aspect of the standard.

Similarly, officials at four of the entities we selected told us they generally have not used performance measures to demonstrate the need to obligate funds for facility security and make appropriate decisions for allocating resources, as is specified in the ISC standard. As with the cost-effectiveness aspect of the standard, this is positive and represents a rigorous approach to using performance measurement in the security environment. These officials said that while they have implemented various types of performance measures, such as tracking the operability of CCTV cameras, they generally do not systematically use such measures for resource allocation decisions to the degree specified by the ISC. Entity officials told us they found it challenging to develop and implement measures related to security because of the complexity of measuring an enhancement's impact on security. Officials from GSA, SSA, and the Smithsonian told us it is difficult to assess whether or not an enhancement has improved security because it is difficult to determine if that enhancement prevented a potential security event, which is similar to a challenge we found in past work looking at facility protection efforts of federal agencies.[49] While this perspective is understandable, we have reported, that in lieu of tracking actual security events, conducting inspections and tests are useful in ensuring adequate levels of protection.[50] Furthermore, these activities could be used to inform resource allocation decisions. For example, testing of security screening, and tracking results, could aid in determining how to allocate resources for technology and screener training. Additionally, our past work has also identified a range of other performance measures used by organizations outside of the U.S. government for facility protection that federal agencies may consider using.[51] Nevertheless, similar to the cost-effectiveness aspect of the ISC standard, officials from GSA, SSA, Smithsonian, and FEMA told us that it would be beneficial for the ISC to provide them with further guidance or examples of how to implement a performance-measurement and testing program that would inform resource allocation decisions.

---

[49]GAO-06-612

[50]GAO-05-49

[51]GAO-06-612

Guidance Needed to Implement ISC Standard on Cost-effectiveness and Performance Measurement

As we noted in a previous report, ISC views one of its primary roles as being the nucleus of communication on key practices and lessons learned for the facility protection community in the federal government and has embraced this responsibility.[52] As such, we discussed the entities' views of the cost-effectiveness and performance measurement aspects of the ISC standard with a senior ISC official, who agreed that these were areas that could be improved. In fact, this official said that an ISC initiative in development might provide an opportunity for such improvements. In the 2012 GAO survey described earlier, federal entities identified allocating resources as their greatest challenge, as well as determining the cost-effectiveness of the technologies they implement. We recommended that DHS direct ISC to help entities make the most efficient use of resources for physical security and develop and disseminate guidance on management practices for resource allocation. In response to this recommendation, ISC created the Resource Management Working Group to identify, compile, and disseminate resource management best practices that entities can use on a voluntary basis. Based on the working group's findings, the ISC drafted guidance describing these best practices, guidance that ISC officials told us is currently undergoing review by its members. As of the end of this review, this guidance was not finalized and so, the extent to which it would contain guidance on determining cost-effectiveness and measuring performance, to the degree specified by the ISC standard, was not known. However, the ISC official said that GAO's work for this report could provide the impetus for developing guidance in these areas in conjunction with this effort.

In developing such guidance, ISC could draw upon several sources to inform decisions about what the guidance could entail and how it could be implemented. Regarding cost-effectiveness, OMB has provided guidance for conducting cost-effectiveness analyses to promote effective resource allocation by the federal government.[53] The guidance describes elements that should be included in this type of analysis, such as establishing the rationale for what is being evaluated, an evaluation of alternatives, and an evaluation of the expected benefits and costs. It also describes guidelines

---

[52]GAO-05-49.

[53]OMB, *Guidelines and Discount Rates for Benefit-Cost Analysis of Federal Programs,* Circular No. A-94 (Washington, D.C.: Oct. 29, 1992). OMB defines cost-effectiveness as a systematic quantitative method for comparing the costs of alternative means of achieving the same stream of benefits or a given objective.

for entities to consider when identifying such benefits and costs. With regard to performance measurement and testing and their relationship to resource allocation, our past work on this topic may serve as a source of information to inform ISC guidance. For example, in 2004, we found that, as part of broad program goals, performance measures could indicate whether organizations establish timelines and adhere to budgets. And, at the individual facility level, on-site security assessments and other active testing could provide data on the effectiveness of efforts to reduce a facility's vulnerability to attack. In this same report, we also noted that key practices include allocating resources using risk management; leveraging security technology; and measuring program performance and testing security initiatives, among other things.[54] Additionally, in 2006, we found a range of examples of performance measures that organizations outside the U.S. government, including private-sector firms, state and local governments, and foreign government agencies, use to help improve the security of facilities, inform risk-management and resource-allocation decisions, and hold security officials and others in their organizations accountable for security performance. These included output measures, such as the average time to process background screenings, and outcome measures, such as the change in the total number of security incidents relating to thefts, vandalism, and acts of terrorism.[55]

As discussed earlier, there is no government-wide data on total amounts expended on facility protection. The multiple funding sources used and the integration of physical security enhancements into other types of projects hinders the identification of total government-wide costs. As such, it is critical that federal entities are equipped with oversight mechanisms to determine the cost-effectiveness of their security investments, and to measure the impact of these enhancements to inform future resource allocation decisions. Without these mechanisms, entities may have insufficient information (1) to evaluate whether the benefits of security investments justify their costs, (2) to know the extent to which security enhancements have improved security or reduced federal facilities' vulnerability to acts of terrorism or other forms of violence, or (3) to determine funding priorities within and across agencies.

---

[54]GAO-05-49.

[55]GAO-06-612.

Conclusions

Since September 11, 2001, federal entities have made improvements to the physical security of their buildings by implementing enhancements to their facilities' interior space, security operations and administration, structure, security systems, entrances, and sites. These enhancements likely have amounted to significant costs to the federal government. Given that it is not fully known how much entities expend on enhancements and that cost factors vary by facility, it becomes an even more essential key practice that entities at both the headquarters and facility levels have the tools necessary to make sound resource allocation decisions. Such tools could help entities understand the effectiveness an enhancement may have on improving security, and help ensure that the benefits of an enhancement outweigh the costs. ISC's risk management standard places an emphasis on assessing cost-effectiveness and measuring performance as part of a rigorous risk management approach for effective resource allocation. While this approach is positive, selected federal entities have had difficulty implementing these aspects of the standard. ISC is well positioned, especially with its working group on resource allocation, to provide entities with guidance to help them implement the cost-effectiveness and performance measurement aspects of its standard. Improvements in these areas could enable federal entities to better determine the benefits of security investments and whether they have reduced federal facilities' vulnerability to acts of terrorism or other forms of violence.

Recommendation for Executive Action

We recommend that the Secretary of Homeland Security direct that ISC, in consultation with ISC members, develop guidance for helping federal entities implement the cost-effectiveness and performance-measurement aspects of ISC's risk management standard. The guidance could be incorporated into ongoing ISC initiatives related to resource allocation, or into other ISC guidance materials, as ISC deems appropriate.

Agency Comments

We provided a draft of this report to DHS, SSA, DOJ, Smithsonian, GSA, OMB, and the AOUSC for review and comment. DHS concurred with the recommendation directed at ISC. DHS stated that ISC is currently developing improved guidance to help agencies make the most effective use of resources available for physical security across the portfolio of facilities. DHS's official written response is reprinted in appendix II. SSA agreed with the report as written and did not have any technical comments. DOJ conveyed its concurrence with the report in an e-mail. DHS, the Smithsonian, and the AOUSC provided technical comments, which we incorporated as appropriate. GSA agreed with the report as

GAO-15-444 Homeland SecurityError! Reference source not found.

written and did not have any technical comments. OMB did not provide any comments on the report.

We are sending copies of this report to the Secretaries of Homeland Security, Justice, and the Smithsonian Institution; the Administrator of the General Services Administration; the Commissioner of the Social Security Administration; the Director of the Administrative Office of U.S. Courts; and the Director of the Office of Management and Budget. In addition, the report is available at no charge on the GAO website at http://www.gao.gov.

If you or your staff have any questions about this report, please contact me at (202) 512-2834 or GoldsteinM@gao.gov. Contact points for our Offices of Congressional Relations and Public Affairs may be found on the last page of this report. GAO staff who made key contributions to this report are listed in appendix III.

Sincerely yours,

Mark L. Goldstein
Director, Physical Infrastructure Issues

Appendix I: Objectives, Scope, and Methodology

The objectives in our review were to identify (1) the types of physical security enhancements that selected civilian federal entities have made to their facilities since September 11, 2001; (2) how selected federal entities pay for and track costs of such enhancements, and the factors that drive those costs; and (3) the actions, if any, that selected civilian federal entities have taken to manage costs, including determining the cost-effectiveness of enhancements and the use of performance measures. Our focus was buildings and excluded structures such as utility systems, roads and bridges, parking structures, and land assets. We also excluded "critical infrastructure," such as dams and national monuments, because these are uniquely protected and their security is addressed through other GAO work.

This report is a public version of a previously issued report identified by the Department of Homeland Security (DHS) and the Department of Justice (DOJ) as containing information designated as For Official Use Only, information that must be protected from public disclosure. Therefore, this report omits sensitive information regarding specific building information, the names and locations of the buildings we visited, among other things. However, the information provided in this report addresses the same questions as the For Official Use Only report, and the overall methodology used for both reports is the same.

To help inform our research, we reviewed and summarized information from reports and documentation on physical security enhancements that have been made across all federal facilities, including any available government-wide data on costs, and interviewed officials familiar with this issue area. For example, we examined prior reports from GAO and the Congressional Research Service, entity submissions to the Office of Management and Budget's (OMB) annual Homeland Security Mission Funding, entity budget requests and appropriations related to security, and documentation from the Interagency Security Committee (ISC), including physical security standards developed by the ISC, such as the ISC's 2013 "The Risk Management Process for Federal Facilities: An Interagency Security Committee Standard." We also interviewed officials from GSA, ISC, and OMB to provide us with a government-wide perspective on these issues.

We selected five entities that (1) hold— and manage the security of—their facilities; (2) lease facilities through GSA and rely on security provided at those facilities; and/or (3) provide security services to building tenants. These entities implemented physical security enhancements at federal facilities since September 11, 2001. The entities we selected

GAO-15-444 Homeland SecurityError! Reference source not found.

include: DHS's Federal Emergency Management Agency (FEMA), the General Services Administration (GSA), DOJ's United States Marshals Service (USMS), the Smithsonian Institution (Smithsonian), and the Social Security Administration (SSA). We selected USMS because it has the primary responsibility for protecting the judiciary, and the judiciary is one of GSA's largest tenants. At each of the five entities selected, we interviewed officials at the entities' headquarters and collected documentation from them on the management of physical security across their facilities, including entities' policies, guidance, and reports on security and asset management and memorandums of understanding describing security stakeholders' roles and responsibilities.

To provide us with examples relevant to our review, we selected 10 facilities that were held or leased by the five selected entities in three geographical areas—Dallas, Texas, Los Angeles, California, and Washington, D.C. We identified facilities that (1) have been renovated or constructed or have had significant expenditures on physical-security since September 11, 2001, (2) whose design included enhanced or unique physical security enhancements due to heightened security concerns, and (3) provided examples of challenges or leading practice of cost management and/or use of performance measures. To ensure a diversity of facilities, we included both single and multi-tenant buildings, buildings where the entity did and did not occupy the majority of space, and those secured by the Federal Protective Service (FPS) and other security organizations, such as the USMS. We relied on building information provided to us by entity officials to make these selections and building data from fiscal year 2012 and 2013 Federal Real Property Profile (FRPP) database and FRPP summary reports.

We interviewed officials responsible for security at these locations and conducted site visits to eight of these facilities.[1] For example, we spoke with GSA building managers at the five selected buildings that were owned or leased through GSA, and the Facility Security Committee (FSC) chair at each of the three multi-tenant buildings we visited. We also spoke with FPS officials at five of the buildings and USMS officials at two of the

---

[1] We did not visit the Smithsonian's National Museum of African American History and Culture because it was under construction and we did not visit the SSA's Alta Mesa Office building because a recent facility assessment included recent photographs of enhancements. We collected sufficient information during our interview with facility officials.

buildings we selected where they provided security services. We were not
able to generalize the information we collected across all civilian federal
agencies because we limited our review to five civilian federal agencies
and 10 selected buildings.

To identify the types of security enhancements that civilian federal entities
have made to their facilities since September 11, 2001, we interviewed
ISC officials and summarized information from ISC standards to identify
and categorize the types of enhancements made across civilian federal
facilities. We also interviewed headquarters officials from the five selected
entities and facility officials about the types of physical security
enhancements they have made at their facilities since September 11,
2001, the types of guidance they used to make these selections, and how
they used ISC guidance. In addition, we reviewed documentation that
described the enhancements they have made in buildings, such as facility
risk assessments, FSC meeting minutes, records of implemented
enhancements, and entities' security policies. We used this information,
along with photographs taken at site visits, to describe each of the
identified categories of enhancements and the reasons for why entities
may implement enhancements above what is recommended by the ISC
or why they may reject an ISC-recommended enhancement.

To understand how selected entities pay for and track the costs of
enhancements, we analyzed information from interviews with the
headquarters officials at the five selected entities about how they fund
enhancements and track the costs of enhancements, and reviewed
documentation they provided us, including budget reports and available
cost data. Using this information, we identified and categorized the means
of funding that the five selected entities used to pay for enhancements
and obtained examples from the 10 selected facilities and site visits of the
enhancements paid for by using these means of funding. We also
described the extent to which entities can identify how much was
expended on enhancements for each of the means of funding used. To
describe the factors that drive costs, we summarized information and
presented examples obtained from interviews with the headquarters
officials at the five selected. We determined that a data reliability
assessment was not needed for this data since the data are used as
context in our review and do not materially affect our findings.

To determine the actions the selected federal entities have taken to
manage costs and use performance measures, we summarized
information collected through interviews with headquarters officials at the
selected entities on the methods used to ensure the enhancements that

are implemented across their facilities are cost-effective and whether they use performance measures to evaluate the effectiveness of those enhancements or for resource allocation decisions. Similarly, we asked facility officials to describe and provide us with documentation, such as any analysis conducted, and cost-effective strategies they used to select or recommend enhancements at their facilities. We also asked them if they use performance measures to evaluate how well enhancements work at their facilities and whether they use such information when determining the enhancements needed. Additionally, we asked headquarters officials at the selected entities and facility officials about the challenges they face or examples of leading practices related to their efforts to manage costs and use performance measures. We then compared their actions to the recommendations in the ISC's 2013 standard that entities should perform cost-effective analyses and implement and use performance measures in their resource allocation decisions. We also interviewed ISC officials about their current efforts to improve entities' management of physical security resources. Additionally, we reviewed other resources available from OMB and GAO that describe the importance of conducting these activities and that provide guidance on how these activities should be conducted.

We conducted this performance audit from January 2014 to March 2015 in accordance with generally accepted government auditing standards. Those standards require that we plan and perform the audit to obtain sufficient, appropriate evidence to provide a reasonable basis for our findings and conclusions based on our audit objectives. We believe that the evidence obtained provides a reasonable basis for our findings and conclusions based on our audit objectives.